FIRSTMATTERPRESS
Portland, Ore.

IT'S JUST YOU & ME, MISS MOON

Copyright © 2021 by Emily Moon
All rights reserved

This is a work of fiction. Any resemblance to actual events or persons, living or dead, is entirely coincidental

Second Edition

The First Edition of this poetry collection was titled "It's Just You & Me, Mr. Moon" and the author's name was Peter Hamer. This fully updated edition affirms the gender of Emily Moon, a transgender poet.

Published in the United States
by First Matter Press
Portland, Oregon

Paperback ISBN 978-1-7338246-9-9

Edited by Lauren Paredes, Andra Vltavín, Caroline Wilcox Reul & Ash Good

Cover Illustration
Copyright © 2020 by Sara Swoboda
@continuousdrawingproject

Book design & typography
by Ash Good www.ashgood.com

FIRSTMATTERPRESS.ORG

IT'S JUST YOU & ME, MISS MOON

emily moon

FIRSTMATTERPRESS
Portland, Ore.

WELDON KEES

American poet, painter, literary critic, novelist, playwright, jazz pianist, short story writer, and filmmaker.

1914 — 1955?

"Weldon Kees was born in Beatrice, Nebraska and attended Doane College, the University of Missouri and the University of Nebraska, earning his degree in 1935. In addition to writing, Kees was passionate about painting and throughout his life created many forms of art including experimental films. In 1955 Kees took his sleeping bag and his savings account book and disappeared, leaving his car on the Golden Gate Bridge. It is not known whether he killed himself or went to Mexico." —*Poetry Foundation*

POEMS

- *11* Almost Too Hyphenate
- *15* Location Is a Character
- *17* The Monkey Room
- *19* Merely Mirrored
- *21* Summer 1946
- *23* The Eyes and Ears of the World
- *26* A Poem in His Fist
- *28* Salt Lime
- *29* The Golden West
- *32* I Like Ike
- *34* It Just Might Be Worth It
- *37* A Late Act
- *39* Spinning
- *41* Just Because We Can't Explain...
- *43* Benzedreaming
- *46* A Foggy Night in San Francisco
- *48* Deeper and Deeper
- *51* Every Nut in San Francisco

52	Oaxaca Zócalo
54	Gringo en Mexico
56	Marooned Somewhere
59	The Queens Arms
61	Into the Sunset
63	Trout Fishing in San Francisco
65	Orange Sunshine
68	July 1976
70	Vision of Frida
71	Acapulco Nightmare
74	A Meeting in Rome
80	Mysterious Kitchens
84	Weldon's Ghost
86	Socially Distant
88	Toynbee or Luminol?
90	Notes
92	Acknowledgments

ALMOST TOO HYPHENATE

Weldon,
typing in his Filbert Street apartment
in San Francisco.
He's working on his third book of poetry.
It will be rejected
22 times.

On the table:
a can with 800 feet of film,
a Rolleiflex, a Leica.
12 envelopes of negatives.
Brushes in a jar of mineral spirits.
Smoke spirals from a cigarette
in the ashtray.

There's a folio of album covers
he's designing
for jazz records.
An unfinished abstract painting
waits on an easel.

An upright piano in the other room.
Jazz wants to fly from the fingers
that pound the typewriter.
He unconsciously strikes
a syncopated rhythm.

In his apartment,
he creates a collage
with letters culled from newspapers.
It will be part of a solo show
in New York City
that will result
in one sale.

Across town,
he collaborates to produce a psychology book.
Sometimes,
he thinks he should be one of its subjects.

He works with an anthropologist
on a study of play.
You can see him interviewing Becky,
a ventriloquist's dummy.
Becky is incredibly incisive.

The can on the table
contains footage for *Hotel Apex*,
an experimental film
he's creating at a derelict flophouse.

The photos in the envelope
are of rooms in people's homes
taken for non-verbal clues in furniture arrangements,
research for a book
he's working on with Jurgen Reusch.
Next year, it will be released with his name
on the cover as a co-author.
He will never see the book.

The fan puffs
open the drapery regularly
in its oscillations.
Beyond the window,
the street is grey-shaded
by lamplight.
It appears almost innocent.

The phone rings.
Weldon continues typing.
He struggles to create art
for a future that looks
as empty and bleak
as the present.

Ann answers the phone
with empty chatter for the other end of the line.

His muse never blinks,
never betrays what she thinks,
never lets on what she knows
about the footsteps echoing
down the long corridor
of eternity.

LOCATION IS A CHARACTER

Weldon walks from the beach
at Provincetown
after smoking marijuana
with Kahlil Gibran Jr.
He feels lightheaded and giddy.
Evening breeze blows offshore,
waves whisper their secrets.
Darkness rises over the Atlantic,
chases the late summer sun
behind his bungalow.

He feels amorous.
Walks through the door,
pours a glass of bourbon,
puts an old jazz record on the phonograph,
flops down on the sofa,
feet on the coffee table,
bopping to the music.

It's quarter past midnight.
Ann is still out.
His amorous feelings do not dissipate.
He is about to take matters into his own hands
when Ann stumbles in,
three sheets to the wind.

Slams the door.
Oops she says.
She stumbles to the bedroom,
kicks off her heels.

Things weren't exactly great between them,
but they'd been worse.
Weldon helps her with her dress,
guides her to the toilet,
wipes her face with a washcloth.
Puts an arm around her shoulder,
walks her to the bed,
pulls the covers up,
turns out the light.

The effects of the marijuana are gone.
On his third bourbon,
he slaps another platter on the turntable,
Fats Waller.
He unbuttons his shirt,
lies back on the couch,
looks at the Full Wolf Moon
through the slats of the blinds. Says
it's just you & me, Miss Moon.
Just you & me.

THE MONKEY ROOM

Huge plate glass windows afford
an opulent view of the tony patrons within.

Who's Who dines here
for the *to be seen scene.*

A large window behind the bar reveals
a troop of spider monkeys

droll in their appeal.
Elegant waiters serve up

extravagant meals with posh theatricality.
Fashionable lounge jazz

mingles with Ivy League accents.
Weldon enters by chance,

requests a table for one.
He's shown to the corner

at the dim end of the windows.
The aroma of regarded clam chowder

thick as fog in the room.
Weldon orders a bowl and a scotch.

Although he's alone,
two cigarettes glow in the ashtray.

A gaggle of pedestrians gawk and point in the window.
Though no gaze lingers on him,

he feels exotic as a spotted lizard.
Sees a familiar form through the window.

I'll be goddamned if it isn't Robinson!
Tosses a bill on the table, downs the scotch,

grabs his hat. Leaves the two cigarettes,
pushes against the current of people

to where Robinson stood.
Finds only the crowd.

MERELY MIRRORED

A bright warm afternoon in the city.
Dead-end alley, shadowed and cool.
Kids pitch pennies against a greasy brick wall.
A slender mustachioed man in a fedora
walks past,

walks backwards two steps, leans back,
peers down the alley.
Something caught his eye, a shadow,
the shape of a man moving.

He scans the alley, looks up
to the rectangle of silky blue. He squints,
looks to the shadows again, sees nothing.
Puts a finger to his lips,
continues on his way.

Weldon walks past
a diner, catches a reflection
in the window, stops sharply, looks around.
Whoever it was is lost in the endless
stream of pedestrians.

Words for a poem start to form in his mind.
He takes out a handkerchief, wipes his brow.
A small notebook is produced
from an inside pocket. People river around him
like trout around an islet. He jots a few notes,
returns the book to the pocket,

walks home to his apartment. He pours a
tumbler of gin, rolls a Bull Durham, spools
a sheet of paper into the typewriter.
Cigarette dangling from the corner of
his mouth, he starts typing.

Robinson, he begins.

SUMMER 1946

Beginning to think of himself
as a serious artist,
Weldon works in his home studio.
Meticulously groomed:
hair honed to a fine sheen,
mustache neatly trimmed,
wing tips shined, undershirt splotched
with color where he wipes his fingers.

Smoke drifts toward the ceiling
from the cigarette poised
at the corner of his mouth.
He thinks his apartment
is one Robinson would like.

Thumb hooked on a palette,
stained ochre, umber, carmine,
brush balanced like a single chopstick,
eyes on the easel.
Applies brush to canvas,
attempts to evoke a sense
of sardonic gloom.

Sips Jack Daniels from a tumbler,
turns back to the abstract on the easel,
adjusts the canvas to catch
the moving sunlight.
He sees something new
in the painting,
something like
a reflection.

THE EYES AND EARS OF THE WORLD

Speaking to a reporter about his job.

I'm a newsreel scriptwriter at Paramount.
The job involves every step of production
from viewing raw footage

to working lines with narrators.
The work itself is formulaic and tedious.
Best thing about the job is

the collaborative nature of the process—
how writers, directors, actors, editors, and cameramen
strive to make quality film. It's an art.

And this job allows me time to work
on my writing while at the office.
A lot of the stuff we produce is pretty lowbrow.

The brass wanted me to do a script
for a Madison Square Garden rodeo
since I'm from "out west." I turned to Andy.

I can't write this shit. You write it.
Under oath, we get material from the Rotapol
war cameramen. We can't talk

about certain things with our friends and loved ones.
Ann is sure agents follow me around. I dunno,
maybe she's right. Just the other day

I noticed a guy in a trench coat
who seemed to be watching me. When I glanced at him,
he took a sudden interest in a window display.

Excuse me I'm dying for a cigarette.
[lights cigarette and exhales] Ahh!
The roughest watch

was the raw Iwo Jima footage.
Untold numbers of Marines and Japanese soldiers died.
Worked day and night to get that one in the can.

After the final edit, Jim called the team around him.
*We have produced one of the best
and most terrible war films.*

It left me sickened and exhausted.
No surprise the Signal Corps had us cut a lot of material.
The American people can't handle it.

That footage is exactly
what the American people need to see.
I can't forget those images.

Well, gin and tonic helps.
I'm heading to Marnell's on East 47th.
Join me for a drink, won't you?

A POEM IN HIS FIST

The night half-hidden
by mercury light.

Drips and ticks ricochet
off grimy brick walls.

Mingled aromas
of moldering trash,
and unwashed bodies.

A shadow figure grows
and twists with the headlights
of a turning car.

Grit crackles under Weldon's
leather soles.

Footsteps click closer.

He turns, a poem in his fist
raised high like a torch.

Robinson?

Dumpster echo, a kicked can,
a scurry of rats.

The shadow flies.

SALT LIME

Tumbler in front of him,
rimmed with salt.
He squeezes lime into the glass.
Dust motes float before his eyes
in patterns that suggest impending doom,
his daily affliction.
He thinks of suicide,
how he once held
a pearled Derringer to his head.
Pulled the trigger.
Stopped his breath.
No bullets in the twin barrels.

THE GOLDEN WEST

Pausing in Portland
on their way to Seattle,
they check into their hotel.
It has rained for weeks.
Ann is tired.
She settles into the easy chair
with a novel and a fifth of gin.

Weldon pulls his overcoat close.
Dons his gray fedora,
hoofs it to the jazz club
at the Golden West Hotel.
During a break,
he schmoozes with the band.
They invite him
to sit in on piano.

He pounds out Fats Waller
while the band soars.
Buzzed with the joy of connection,
he scans his fellow musicians,
locks eyes
with the man on drums.

Fireworks go off in his head,
the heat of lust in those eyes.
Consumed by a confusion of emotions,
he is embarrassed
by his erection.
Turns away as he works the piano
to a stumbling climax.

Thanked by the band,
he shuffles out
into the shimmered streets.
He wanders over a bridge,
pauses midspan,
lights a cigarette
and stares into the river.

Thinks about other bridges,
bridges from verse to chorus,
piano to drums.
Bridges high enough for a leap
into cold dark water.

He heaves a sigh,
tosses the butt into the river.

Goes straight to his room,
snuggles into bed,
spoons Ann.
His eyes wide open,
staring into the darkness
in her hair.

I LIKE IKE

Morning.
The light serves only to emphasize
the dust that settles on everything
like a veneer of progress.

Casual insanity is everywhere.
He's sure the fascists
are winning.
Depression seems
like a reasonable response.

Hat at a jaunty angle,
Weldon angles out the door for work.
Sick of the job,
needs the cash.

He's proudest of his work
on the Bikini atomic blast newsreel.
Thinks it ironic
or prophetic
the provocative two-piece swimsuit
is named for a place of immense destruction.

On the bus,
a man stares at him.
Weldon turns away.
Boosted by the attention,
he gets off at his stop
with a lilt in his step.

At the office,
he doffs his hat with flair,
looks around,
sees everyone is wearing
an *I Like Ike* button.

Goddamn fascists, he thinks.
Good morning, he says pleasantly.

IT JUST MIGHT BE WORTH IT

Weldon wakes sweating and shaking,
fixated by the eyes!

He dreamt he was a praying mantis.
He and a female proceeded
to do what animals have done
from time primeval.
At the point of orgasm,
her face turned to his
and she fixed him with her eyes.

He stared back helplessly,
feeling strangely ecstatic and terrified.
In a swift move, she bit off his head!
His body convulsed in spasms,
which elevated their pleasure immensely.
He was caught in a swirl
of bliss and dread.

Heart racing,
breathing heavily,
he checks the radium dial of his watch.

Gets up, splashes cold water
on his face,

pulls back the drapes,
looks out the window.
The cold moon hangs over the city.

He lights a cigarette,
considers the fate
of the male mantis.
Ponders if losing one's head
is worth a night
of great sex.

He ponders a few moments,
puffs thoughtfully.
Shakes his head.
Nah, not worth it.

He tamps out his cigarette,
rubs his eyes,
reclines back into bed.

Phosphenes cross the velvet dark
behind his eyelids.
He reflects on his life.
Feels the weight of his sleeping wife.

Mulls his brushes with success and fame,
a sad succession of disappointments.

He slams open his eyes,
stares into the darkness.
Goddamn, he thinks. *Yes. Yes!*
It just. Might. Be. Worth it!

A LATE ACT

The scene opens.
Pink light under clouds.
Rocks on the shore.
Clumps of decaying seaweed.
Skittering birds.
Beach walkers hug themselves.

Houses light up one by one.
A girl sings *Miss Susie had a baby* . . .
Wind blows off shore, dragging night behind.
Salt air. Aromas of suppertime.

Pan up the coast in deepening dusk.
A North Beach café.
Diners dine. Drinkers drink.

Focus on a couple seated at a corner table in the back.
Food unfinished, the man orders another gin and tonic.

The woman's eyes red rimmed.
An overpowering perfume.
Note a tissue in her hand.
She leans across the table,
reaches for the man's hand.

His hand moves away. He stares at the table.

She cries into her napkin.
Diners glance at the couple. We hear their whispers.
A waiter delivers the cocktail.

Weldon feels the looks, hears the hushed hubbub.
He pays up, leaves a generous tip, quaffs the drink.
He dons his fedora with a brisk move.
I'll be waiting. Exits to the car.

Ann sits for a bit, mystified.
What *is* she going to do?
She finishes her vodka.
Goes to the lady's room.
Washes her face, freshens her makeup.
Joins her husband in the car.

She dabs her eyes with a handkerchief,
while they drive toward the Presidio.
He drops her at a friend's place.
Enjoys the quiet ride back to his apartment.

SPINNING

Muggy summer evening, an apartment
somewhere in San Francisco. Ann

is in the asylum. *I Love Lucy* bleats
from the tube. Wind from the window

carries the scent of the bay. Weldon slouches
in his chair, wearing undershirt, boxers, slippers,

knees bouncing, drinking gin. Canned lines
from the TV disgust him. He slips

into a reverie. Televised laughter fades
away. He imagines air rushing,

water approaching, then a slam
that feels like heat, followed by cold.

He goes down... down...
light fades...

Sudden laughter bursts through.
He jerks, startled. The TV blares.

He turns down the volume, staggers
into the bathroom, looks at the image

in the flecked mirror.
Splashes cold water on his face,

slugs down a couple bennies. In the living
room, he lights a cigarette, pours more gin,

turns out the lights. Flickering images
from the round tube

cast a ghostly glow. Ann is still
in the asylum. Something like remorse

or relief flickers at the edge of thought.
He sits at the piano, knees jumping,

pounds out "Holiday Rag" too fast.
Then plays it again, faster...

JUST BECAUSE WE CAN'T EXPLAIN . . .

Weldon driving toward Mount Tamalpais.
A bright, pulsing light descends and hovers
in front of his Mercury Zephyr.
The headlights go out,
the motor quits.
He stomps the gas pedal,
turns and turns the key
while the car fades to a stop.

Watching the light, he gets out,
raises his fanned hand to shade his eyes,
thinking *What the . . .*
A pale blue beam extends,
pulls him up and in.

In a windowless, wedge-shaped room,
a hollow thrumming fills his head.
People in bulbous gray suits
like atomic workers,
hold mysterious instruments.
He blacks out.

He comes to restrained on a table, naked.
Smells metal and a perfume
he can't quite place.
Lifts his head, squints
to see a silver mechanism
protruding from his navel.
The bright pulsing light
scrunches his eyes
shut.

Thinks he should have
gone through with his plan
to leap from the Golden Gate.

He hears a familiar voice. Ann.
This one, she says,
is mine.

BENZEDREAMING

Weldon, at the podium,
fidgeting. Fingers dance
like a swarm of bees.
Taps his foot.
Accepts an award.

It's a smallish auditorium,
leather seats, walnut paneling.
Several projection windows
glint from the back of the room.
The aroma of pine oil
makes his left eyelid twitch.

He scans the crowd.

Old friends W. H. Auden,
Dr. Williams, Mark Rothko,
Conrad Aiken, present.

Members of the academy
sit in a row
nodding under expensive hats.

*Is that Jimmy Stewart's friend
Harvey in the back row?*
Rubs his eyes, guess not.
That twitch is still going . . .

He squints into the spotlight,
grips the podium.
A pre-migraine aura
obscures an arc of faces.
He leans into the microphone.
I never thought you'd see me here.
Appreciative laughter bubbles up.

He reads selections from his
triumphant third book.
The audience moves
like waves in synchrony
with the cadence
of his film noir voice.

He finishes with a slight bow,
a moderate smile below his
perfectly trimmed moustache.
The audience rises in ovation.

Searching the sea of heads:
Robinson.
Goddam, Robinson, where are you?

The applause seems to be
for someone who isn't here.

A FOGGY NIGHT IN SAN FRANCISCO

Last time I saw Weldon,
it was a foggy night in San Francisco.
I came upon him unexpectedly,
leaning against a lamp post.

Cigar smoke hung like a bent halo.
The lone streetlight cast
a golden nimbus around him.
He wore a dark trench coat and fedora.
It was close to midnight.

Weldon! What's shakin'?
He regarded me,
took a slow drag on his stogie.
Waiting for Robinson. How about you?

Sounds of the harbor clanked around us.
Salt breeze carried a tang of diesel
and sewage.
A clock chimed some ways off.
He checked his watch. Cinderella hour.

One corner of a poster flapped on the lamp post.
I cocked my head toward the rusty freighter
moored alongside the pier.
My ship.

Waves lapped against the hull.
He produced a flask,
took a swig, offered it to me.
Sure, I shrugged.
I tipped it back. Rotgut bourbon.
I felt the burn on my throat.

The Alcatraz foghorn
blew its lonely note.
See ya around.
Yeah, stomping out his cigar.

A gull squawked.
A truck sputtered down the quay.
He checked his watch again.
Goddamn Robinson,
he muttered as I walked away.

I looked back as I
crossed the gangplank.
Only the golden veil
of lamplight remained.

DEEPER AND DEEPER

Late afternoon. Fog rolls in from
the Pacific. He parks his car,
walks out on the Golden Gate Bridge,
leans over the railing, ponders

the four-second drop. Something
diverts him, the sound of the wind,
maybe a wisp of a dream
that refuses to give up on him.

He looks out toward open water
and possibility. He follows
the something across the bridge into
the shrouded city, wanders

the brooding town for hours. His shoes
lead him down Filbert Street,
past his apartment, up Telegraph Hill
to Coit Tower. The bay is deep

in haze. Beacons on the bridge fade
in and out, seem to float in the mist.
He scans the waterfront. Mast
lights shift and shimmer like spirits.

The embers of his corpus
warm him like this evening's chill.
He pulls his trench coat close. Trailing
cigar smoke, he traipses downhill

toward the Embarcadero.
The Alcatraz foghorn moans.
Ships are dewy in dim light.
A lonely sax carries blues down

empty avenues. He meanders
to a familiar bar, orders gin,
sits awhile, sipping and sighing.
Sighing gets the best of him.

He heads out to the abandoned
streets, rambles through the murk alone.
Jumbled thoughts trouble his mind:
Robinson — The Bridge — Mexico.

A ghost of an idea haunts
his cloudy head. It emerges
from his subconscious. Slowly it
becomes a burgeoning urge.

He plods toward the harbor. The purr
of a tug jazzes his step.
He hastens his pace at the slap
of waves between quay and ship.

He beholds tramp steamer Veracruz—
destination: Manzanillo—
departure: imminent. A breeze
sweeps away the haze. The scene glows

with numinous light. He arranges
passage. Soon he is standing
at the rail, beatific, passing
under the Golden Gate, moving

deeper into the fog.

EVERY NUT IN SAN FRANCISCO

I had just purchased a curious little shop
in North Beach. Part bookstore,
part tea room, part occult haven.

We sold incense, astrology books,
had tarot readers, a Brooklyn medium,
a lady with a crystal ball,
a piano in the corner for ambiance.

End of the first day, I'm closing up shop.
Papa Wel, our piano player,
coat over his arm, fedora on cockeyed,
said, *Ya know, sooner or later,*
every nut in San Francisco's gonna walk
through that door.

He donned his overcoat, straightened his hat,
and strode out into the gray night.

OAXACA ZÓCALO

Weldon emerges from his *casita*.
Scrambles with his shades.
Catches a glimpse
of a large, bearded man

lumbering through a narrow door.
A radio blares sudden Mexican jazz.
Robinson!
I thought you were in New York!
Without turning,
the man enters,
closes the door.
The music halts.

He fumbles with his pocket watch.
About 10:30.
Ambles in the afterfog
of a night with Señor Cuervo.

In the *zócalo*,
he sits by the fountain,
relights the cigar drooping
at the corner of his mouth.
He remembers

keys in the ignition,
dust motes in sunlight,
glint on the metal dash,
doors locked.

Children chatter,
fill jugs at the fountain.
He pushes his shades up,
rubs his eyes,
adjusts his glasses.

A spindly cactus growing next to the bench
seems to dance in the breeze.
There is no

breeze.

GRINGO EN MEXICO

The bar: pink and yellow,
ornate door casing.
Chips in the layered paint
reveal bright colors.
A mariachi band romps in a corner.
Smiling señoritas dispense
spiritual salvation.
Villagers dance, drink, laugh,
play cards and dice.

Weldon at an outdoor table,
a string of 25-watt bulbs overhead,
plays poker with ex-pat ex-GIs.
They are beefy, heavy drinking men
accustomed to hard duty.

The drink tonight is tequila.
He examines his hand.
He's got nothing.
His turn to bet.
He unfans his cards,
hears a voice
clear as the ting
from the wedding glass:
Go for it!

Floating on a fleecy mescal cloud,
he appraises the bleary men
around the table,
reads their inscrutable red faces.
The wind picks up.
Annoyed by an off-time accordion,
he thinks hard,
makes a sizable bet.

The lights sway in the breeze.
The dizzy shadows
dance with the lights;
a cloud of smoke drifts over the table,
aroma of roasting meat.
A wave of laughter crests
over the partiers.

The cards laid down, the air stills.
An attractive middle-aged woman,
dressed in the village style,
smiles and poses for him.

He watches his money swept across the table,
looks up,
locks eyes with the alluring woman.
She cocks her head in invitation.

MAROONED SOMEWHERE

A bar with a haphazard
nostalgic ambiance.
Old photographs
pepper the walls,
bowling trophies
gather dust,
a signed baseball has a place of honor
in a glass case above the till.
A silent TV blazes
from an upper corner of the room.
Some old jazz number drifts
from the jukebox in the corner.

It's early in the day.
The bartender wipes the bar
for the umpteenth time,
leans back, studies his fingernails.
The place is empty
except for the couple
sitting at the bar.

She's a garrulous,
middle-aged woman,
dressed as if she popped
in on her way to church.

The slim figure of Weldon
next to her,
chin resting on one hand,
fedora tipped back on his head.
He wears a suit of the sort
a traveling salesman might wear.

She's drinking scotch, beer back.
Without pausing her verbal stride,
she waves at the bartender and points
at the empty shot glass in front of her.
Another shot is decanted
and delivered with expeditious aplomb.
She speaks almost nonstop
in a vague East Coast accent.

Weldon stares into his gin,
slowly rotates his glass,
intermittently listens
to the woman
carry on about some guy she knew.

She tips her shot glass back,
slaps it on the bar,
takes a healthy swig of beer,
wipes her mouth with a floral hankie
extracted from a voluminous handbag.

Yeah, she continues,
he said he knew the president!
He was in the Pacific
during the war.
It was very rough. He was sniper or something.
I met him at an art opening in San Francisco.
He was so gallahnt, fetched a glass of wine for me
every time a waiter walked by. Get this—
once,
he was marooned
on a desert island!

Weldon looked up from his gin,
wearily shook his head. *Robinson,*
Goddamn Robinson!

THE QUEENS ARMS

Weldon trudges streets he used to roam in Manhattan.
He would spend the day with the Brooklyn Bridge,
admire the opera of cable and stone,
look over the railing to the river below,
wonder about currents and tides
and how many seconds from leap to splash.

The day wanes into gray twilight.
Honking taxis travel in schools like yellow fish.
He slips into a bar to avoid the rush-hour crush.

He sets his fedora on the counter,
runs his hand through thinning hair,
glances at the tiny TV tucked into a corner,
the fuzzy image of a late season ballgame on the screen.

The bar fills with alcohol-fueled camaraderie,
conversations rise to a bleak roar.

Weldon sips his lonely drink.
Thinks about bridge jumpers
and near misses.

He exits the bar into the glare of streetlamps.
The crowd thinned out,
collars pulled up against brisk evening air.

He falls into *The Queens Arms,*
a cheap boarding house.
His room is just wide enough
for a twin bed and a small dresser.
Bathroom down the hall.

He tunes the radio to a classical station.
A tenor's voice rises with passion.

A soprano sings an accusation.
The orchestra flares.

Weldon pours himself a bourbon.
Stares out the fly-specked window of his narrow room.
Admires the impressionist view.

The overture rises and climaxes.
Applause.

He thinks of something Robinson said.
Hating opera
is part of loving it.

INTO THE SUNSET

Summer, New Orleans, 1962.

Sunset crept into every street.
Down an alley, someone tossed
an empty bottle against a wall.
The sound of breaking glass
sizzled against the jazz background
and the buzz of conversation.

Weldon strolled with an intensity
in his bearing. He wore a Panama
hat, a Hawaiian shirt, and shades
though it was growing dark.

A stocky bald man in a cheap suit
sat at a sidewalk table.
Weldon spotted him, slowed his pace,
and let out a weary laugh.
Robinson! You old scoundrel!
The man looked at Weldon,
highball glass halfway to his mouth.
Excuse me?

Weldon stared. *Sorry, my mistake.*
He *started* to turn away.
Jay Ronald Lane Latimer.
The man held out his hand.

Weldon, said Weldon,
shaking Latimer's hand.
Call me Latimer, everyone does.
Sit down, have a drink.

Let's get to know each other.
One can never have too many friends.
Weldon plucked the cigar
from his mouth, looked at Latimer.
I'm on my way to meet a lady.
Latimer laughed. *Of course!*
Come by some time and have that drink.

A voice in the bar.
Latimer, phone for you.
He held out his hand,
Here's my card. Call anytime.
Latimer disappeared into the bar.

Weldon disappeared
into the sunset.

TROUT FISHING IN SAN FRANCISCO

Summer, 1962. A shadowless cloudy day.

Weldon's in San Francisco
to see how the old burg was holding up.

He found his way to Washington Square,
sat on a green park bench near the Benjamin
Franklin statue. A girl in a red dress played
in the sandbox. The usual sounds as traffic
bustled down Columbus.

He pushed his fedora back, popped a freshly
rolled Bull Durham in the corner of his mouth,
sparked it to life. Movement at the liquor
store across the street caught his eye.

He observed a tall man with a wild blonde mane
exit the store, cross toward the park, walk straight
to the bench, plop down with a gallon jug. The wild
maned man said, *I've got 8 pounds of wine here.*

Weldon took a final drag on his cig,
looked up the street toward the City Lights Bookstore,
then back at the strange man. He flicked
away the butt. *My name's Weldon.*

Richard's my name, poetry's my game. He
uncorked the wine, and they passed the jug back
and forth, talked about Nelson Algren and Hart Crane
and *Journey to the End of the Night.*

They were last seen
heading up Stockton toward China Town,
the scent of trout steamed
with ginger and shallots drawing them
like an expertly cast fly.

ORANGE SUNSHINE

Orange is like a man convinced of his powers.
—Kandinsky

Weldon shuffled to the hotel bathroom
blinking to unstick his eyes.
The mirror revealed
hair at angles, a light blue pallor,
sore knees, a belly ache.
I'm going to rot like an old car.

Later.
Showered, shaved, perfectly coiffed.
Southern Comfort in his belly,
blue sheen burnished
to the shade of an arctic diamond.
He headed out the door wearing
a banker's shirt, a skinny tie, a tan trilby.
It was 1 PM.

He walked up Fulton St. to Golden Gate Park.
A free concert by the Grateful Dead.
He was curious
about the new kind of music they played.

A sea of colorful young people
wearing jeans and beads,
flowers in their hair,
incense in the air.
Balloons bounced over the crowd.

Someone passed him a joint.
He looked at it for a moment,
took a puff, handed it back.

A young man
offered him a tiny orange cylinder.
What's this? The young man swept
hair from his eyes. *Acid man, Orange Sunshine.*
Let it dissolve under your tongue.
You'll see God.

Weldon learned something about LSD
working at the Langley Porter clinic
the previous decade.
He put the barrel under his tongue.

After 30 minutes or so,
getting into the bop of the music,
he forgot all about it.

The music appeared
as shifting patterns of color
like flashing antic tiles.
Weldon turned to a woman,
tracers followed his focus.
This music is orange.

Far out, she said.

Swaying with the crowd,
he painted the music with his hands
in vibrating arcs.

God failed to make an appearance.

JULY 1976

Weldon is back in the country
for the big birthday bash.
Signs of decay are everywhere.
He's meeting Robinson for dinner in LA.
It's been a while.

He reads the Hotel Law notice
on his room door.
A lot of crap about penalties
for defrauding the hotel,
nothing about penalties
for the hotel defrauding the lodger.

He pauses,
decides to pee again before leaving.
His prostate's been acting up.
Steps into the bright sunshine,
puts on his shades, pulls the brim
of his Panama hat.

From the taxi,
under the overpass,
he sees young people
with spikey hairstyles
wearing leather,
safety pins in their ears.
He thinks, *that looks like*
a fresh wind blowing against the empire.
But what the fuck do I know.

The cab drops him at a posh restaurant.
He leans against a pillar, crosses his arms,
waits for Robinson.

VISION OF FRIDA

Weldon wakes from a dream in his *casita*
in Oaxaca. Ivy grows from his head,

spreads across the sheets. Brightens to a vision
of Frida hovering over her deathbed,

paintbrush in hand. Self-portraits rise
behind her like cards in the Sir John Tennile

Alice in Wonderland drawing. She hands
him the brush, *Tu pintas*. Her back-brace glows

through her bedclothes like something holy:
Our Lady of the Surrealists. She

fades a bit at a time until only
her eyebrows remain. Then, they wink out.

He rubs his eyes, fumbles for a cigarette,
hears strains of 1920s jazz,

alto sax fronting a gang of horns. It's
a long time since his hand held a brush.

ACAPULCO NIGHTMARE

Sunny day. Waves roll in,
sea birds call, palm trees rustle
in the gentle breeze.
Tourists in *el mar*. Some swim,
some play, some stand knee deep
drinking tropical cocktails
through straws in coconuts.

Weldon, sits in the shade
of a beach umbrella,
two paintbrushes in one hand,
palette hooked on the other thumb.
He daubs paint on a canvas
of convenient size to fit
under an airplane seat.
Finished paintings glisten
on a portable rack.

A man with an expansive belly
under a souvenir t-shirt
watches for a time, sipping
from a straw in a coconut.
He approaches,
examines the work.

Weldon looks up,
his face a map of wrinkles.
He's wearing a straw hat
and an unbuttoned gauze shirt
that exposes a slight paunch.
He says *Hola, amigo*.
Goes back to his painting:
a brilliant ruby sun
over a shining teal sea
with pistachio green bathers
on a lilac beach.

These aren't too bad.
He looks up again, squints,
recognizes an old acquaintance
from the San Francisco art scene.

Weldon takes a healthy swig
from a thermos of margaritas
They talk about time,
the sea, the art exhibit Weldon's
organizing with his *campañeros*.

They haggle over a sunset
and palm trees rendered
in mauve, turquoise,
and banana yellow.
He wraps it in cardboard,
ties it up with twine.
All smiles, they shake hands,
slap each other's backs.
Nice to see you.

Weldon sits down feeling
queasy. *Once*, he thinks,
I was an artist.

A MEETING IN ROME

He arrived from Paris via train
the night before. He was in Rome
to meet Robinson at Sergio's,
a pub near the Vatican.
Dusk was settling in when heard
the sputtering neon sign.
He thought, *Just the kind of place
Robinson would like.*

He passed through the door,
looked around. The room
was a narrow, comfortable place.
Oak interior, no mirror behind the bar.
It held the sour aroma of stale beer
and cigarette smoke. A radio
played cheesy Italian jazz.

There was just enough room
for three or four petite round tables
along the wall opposite the bar.
A few paintings embellished the wall.
The dark light and yellowed paint
made it impossible to make out their subjects.

A couple held hands at a table,
leaned close in a way that was
almost religious. A disheveled man
in a soiled Armani suit
brooded over a half-empty pint glass
at the furthest end of the bar
where the room dissolved into shadow.

Weldon took a stool midway
down the bar. He nodded to the bartender,
ordered gin and tonic, lit up a Gauloises
from the pack he bought in Paris.
He was smoking thoughtfully
when a man in a bishop's cape walked in,
sat next to him, and held up a finger.
Buenas noches, Sergio.
The barman efficiently served up scotch
on the rocks. The bishop raised the glass
to Weldon, *Salud!* He downed the scotch
at once. *Ahhh!* He raised his finger again.
Sergio decanted another shot
of twelve-year-old scotch,
removed the empty, wiped the counter,
and delivered the fresh shot
without seeming to move much at all.

The man turned to Weldon and said,
I'm Pope Francis.

Weldon glanced at him, sat
a little straighter on his stool.
Pleased to meetcha, Father. I'm Weldon.

The Pope raised his hand and made
the familiar sign of blessing.
Bless you, my son.

Weldon nodded. *Thanks.
I didn't know you were a drinking man.*

*Sometimes a good shot of Scotch
salves the soul.* He shrugged.
*There's always a cardinal at my elbow
relating issues of great importance
or urging me to go somewhere
or to sign something.*

When I can, I slip away to this little place.
He circled his hand to indicate the bar,
fell into reverie.

After a few moments, he said,
The bartender, he's an old amigo
from Buenos Aires.

Weldon raised his glass to the bartender.
Sergio raised his eyebrows in acknowledgement,
continued polishing glasses.
So what does the Pope do
when not doing church business?

Listen to classical music, read poetry.
I'm a student of Italian postwar films.
He sipped from his glass.

A film buff! The neorealists.
Now, their films were true.
Weldon raised his glass in salute.

Ah, yes, yes, said the Pope.
Ordinary people as actors, the countryside,
rundown cities as sets.

Weldon nodded. *You know the film* Paisan?
Who was that illiterate actress . . . Carmen . . . ?

Carmela Sazio.
Rossellini threw away the script,
let her natural ability
shine. Hard to believe
she was not a professional.
The pontiff sipped thoughtfully.
So, what brings you to Rome?

Me? Well, I'm meeting an old friend.

Just about that time,
a couple of cardinals rushed in.
They gestured a pantomime of their discussion,
pointed in a direction that might be north.
Their bobbing heads
whispered something in Latin.
The Pope looked at Weldon and sighed.
Excuse me. He raised his glass.
Weldon raised his glass—*Salud!*
and they downed them together.
Good talking with you, Weldon.

Likewise, Father.

The cardinals escorted the Pope out of the bar.
Nice guy, said Weldon to the bartender,
raised his glass for a refill.
Nothing like what I expected.

The barman,
as an angel might,
poured gin and tonic into a clean glass.
He's kind of, uh, regular.

*A guy named Robinson
been here looking for me?*

MYSTERIOUS KITCHENS

words in italics are from Hart Crane's The Bridge

Weldon sits in a small town train station,
unsure of how he came to be in this place,
in this chair. Smell of fresh paint and pine oil,
a cigarette glows in a pedestal
ashtray. He picks up the smoke, inhales
deeply. Mullioned windows

look out on darkness. From unseen speakers,
nonsense announcements in a neutral voice.
eyes like agate lanterns
He tilts his fedora back, could use a drink.
He realizes his clothes are damp.
Chin on hand, elbow on knee, he wonders

"How did my clothes get wet?"
the Bridge is above
"The bay?" He's not sure.
Mysterious kitchens. You shall search them all
He rises, approaches the ticket window,
calls out, "Anyone here?"
A bottle on the counter,
shot glass inverted on the neck.

Only in darkness
He hefts the bottle, returns to his seat,

is thy shadow clear
pours himself a shot. Nice, he thinks, smooth.
A fresh cigarette burns in the ashtray.
He leans back in the chair, ankle on knee,
fedora riding the back of his head,

smokes thoughtfully. Downs another shot.
telepathy of wires submerges an iron year
His thinking clears. So he sits and thinks
back to his apartment: socks soaking
in the bathroom sink, books on the night stand.

Drags on his cig.
Only in darkness
The wind blew up.
Tilting there momentarily, shrill shirt ballooning.
He locked the door,
walked down the block, looked back.
Some inmost sob half heard
Lonesome the cat.
Lonesome, pure heart,
dissuades the abyss
alone in the apartment.
some shore beyond desire!

The sound of someone clearing their throat.
fog insulated noises
Robinson at the far end of the row?
some boding shade
Weldon rises, starts to speak.
nervous shark tooth
The other man turns.
hades in the brain
Disheveled, pupils like black holes.
transmuting silence

Weldon's words stick in his throat.
triggered in the listening vault
He spins, looks around the room,
the empty ticket booth,
the dark window.
Only in darkness

He rushes to the ticket window,
is thy shadow clear
grips the bars, yells "Anyone?"
A door slams.
bending to a scream
Turns, surveys the room. No one is there.

Worlds that glow and sink
Outside, a conductor
cries "All Aboard!"
followed by the sound
of a locomotive gathering steam.

bending to a scream
A fresh cigarette burns in the ashtray.
The bottle is full again.
Bubbles in time
Weldon sits down, wipes his brow,
downs another shot, puffs,
leans back, watches the smoke rise.
dispersed in veils,
Wonders when the next train departs.
the telegraphic night coming on

WELDON'S GHOST

At his old Filbert Street apartment,
Weldon's shade is sometimes seen.

He sports a vest,
an Oxford button down,
brown derby angled
on his precisely combed hair,
mustache neatly trimmed
as in life.

He sits at the ghost
of a Chicago-type bordello piano
and pounds out old Fats Waller tunes.

The cigarette clenched
at the corner of his mouth
leaves no ash. He nods
in time with the music.
Spectral smoke
winds around his head.

A shadowy tangle
of seaweed twists around
his legs. Water pools at his feet.

He drinks the spirit of Jack Daniels
from the highball glass
he sets on the upright of the piano.

A man took a picture of the apparition.
All that was revealed was light
and shade. More shade than light.

SOCIALLY DISTANT

Weldon walks
to the inconvenient
smoking area.
His dark fedora is
fashionable again.

He holds his walking stick
under his arm
as he cups his hands
to light up, success announced
by the bright cherry
as he snaps his Zippo shut.

The only other person
smoking on this cold, rainy day
is a young woman who holds
herself close in a floral cardigan
like she has a force field
surrounding her.
Weldon does not attempt
conversation.

He leans back against
the soiled brick wall.
A passing delivery van

coughs a cloud
of toxic particulates.
Weldon waves the fumes
away as he exhales
a funnel of smoke.

He thinks back to the time
Robinson commandeered
a taxi by convincing
the cabby he was having
a heart attack. Weldon's date
got a kick out of the stunt.
It was funny until Weldon
paid for the ride while Robinson
left with the woman.

Where was that? New Orleans?
San Francisco? Tijuana?
Everything runs together
like paint on a palette.

He checks his watch,
flicks the butt to the gutter.
It's time to go.

TOYNBEE OR LUMINOL?

Weldon ponders which
soporific will be most
effective tonight
for the Snow Moon rises
and Lonesome purrs on his lap

NOTES

"Almost Too Hyphenate": The title is a paraphrase of a statement made by Kathleen Rooney in the Poetry Off the Shelf podcast *Asleep, But Not at Rest*. The list of Weldon's artistic pursuits is from *Vanished Act: The Art and Life of Weldon Kees* by James Reidel.

"The Eyes and Ears of the World" was the slogan for Paramount News. Quotations in the poem come from or are inspired by *Vanished Act*.

"A Poem In His Fist": The title is inspired by the line "Poem in my fist" from *Blk Girl Art* by Jamila Woods.

"Spinning": *Holiday Rag* is a piano composition by Kees.

"Just Because We Can't Explain . . .": Details of the UFO abduction were inspired by *Incident at Exeter* by John G. Fuller.

"Every Nut in San Francisco": In the early 2000s, my wife Julie and I ran Sirius Books and Crafts, a metaphysical shop in Honolulu. One day, David Alvarez, one of our card readers said, as he left the shop, "Sooner or later every nut in Honolulu is going to walk through that door."

"Gringo en Mexico": The title is taken from the Wendy Waldman song of the same title.

"Marooned Somewhere": Details about the gallant gent are from Kees' poem "Robinson at Home."

"Into the Sunset": A sighting of Kees in New Orleans in 1962 is described in *Vanished Act*. Jay Ronald Lane Latimer is an interesting character who revitalized the poetry career of Wallace Stevens. I learned about him from the Poetry Off The Shelf podcast *Modernism's Mystery Man*.

"Trout Fishing in San Francisco": With affection for Richard Brautigan's *Trout Fishing in America*.

"Orange Sunshine": "I'm going to rot like an old car" is from *Vanished Act*.

"Vision of Frida": Special thanks to Chandell Perez for helping me get *Tu pintas* right.

"A Meeting in Rome": The idea for Weldon's meeting with the Pope comes from Kees' poem "Robinson at Home." Information on Pope Francis' hobbies is from *Wikipedia*.

"Mysterious Kitchens": Phrases in italics come from *The Bridge* by Hart Crane; "socks soaking in the sink" is from *Vanished Act*; "books on the nightstand" is from John T. Irwin's superb *The Poetry of Weldon Kees: Vanishing as Presence*.

"Toynbee or Luminol": The title is from Kees' poem "Aspects of Robinson."

ACKNOWLEDGMENTS

It's Just You and Me, Miss Moon is a work of fiction that explores alternative paths for poet and polymath Weldon Kees life and afterlife. I have mined James Reidel's excellent biography *Vanished Act: The Art and Life of Weldon Kees* in writing these poems. I learned about Kees from an interview with poet Kathleen Rooney on the Poetry Foundation's Poetry Off The Shelf podcast *Asleep, But Not at Rest*. I was hooked by the Robinson poems and Kees' story. I am indebted to Curtis Fox, host of the Poetry Off the Shelf podcast series for introducing me to Kees.

I am grateful for OneRoom poetry writing practice group and my poetry coaches Caroline Goodwin, Lauren Hilger, and Hannah Beresford for helping me become a better poet.

Thanks to poets Ralph J. Long Jr., Karine Ancellin, Catherine Martinez, and Rob McCabe for friendship and critiquing some of the poems in this book.

Gratitude and respect for the poets of the Eastside Poetry Workshop for camaraderie and helping me improve my craft. Thanks to Andrew Chenevert, Lauren Paredes, and Caroline Reul for organizing the Eastside meetups.

Sara Swoboda's amazing cover art helps bring this collection to life. Thank you Sara!

Especial thanks to Ash Good, Andra Vltavín, Lauren Paredes and Caroline Reul of First Matter Press. I am grateful for their inspiration, encouragement, and guidance. A budding poet couldn't hope for a better editorial team.

EMILY MOON is a transgender poet. She is co-chair of the Estacada Area Arts Commission, sits on the board of the Performing Arts Group of Estacada, and is the founder of the Estacada Poetry Project. Her work appears in or is forthcoming from *Anti-Heroin Chic, Take a Leap, Spank the Carp*, the *2020 Clackamas County Poets and Artists Calendar, Cæsura* and *A Poet's Agora Confinement Poetry Collection* (in earlier publications under the name Peter Hamer).

FIRSTMATTERPRESS
Portland, Ore.

SELECTED TITLES FROM FIRST MATTER PRESS

BODY UNTIL LIGHT
K.M. Lighthouse

CONSIDER THE BODY, WINGED
Jessica E. Pierce

IT'S JUST YOU & ME, MISS MOON
Emily Moon

LOVERS AND OTHER STILL CREATURES
Eitan Codish

OTHERWISE, MAGIC
Lauren Paredes

ROUTES BETWEEN RAINDROPS
Dan Wiencek

THE GROWTH LINES
Gabby Hancher

THE NIGHT SKY IS A PLACE WHERE THINGS GET LOST
Andrew Chenevert

WE ARE NOT READY FOR WHAT WE ARE
Ash Good

FIRSTMATTERPRESS.ORG

www.ingramcontent.com/pod-product-compliance
Lightning Source LLC
Chambersburg PA
CBHW042319090526
44583CB00025BA/3196